Martín & Meditations
on the South Valley

Jimmy Santiago Baca

Martín & Meditations on the South Valley

INTRODUCTION BY DENISE LEVERTOV

A NEW DIRECTIONS BOOK

Grateful acknowledgement is made to *Imagine: International Chicano
Poetry Journal* (Vol. I, No. 1, Summer 1984), in which sections I & II
of *Martín* first appeared.

Manufactured in the United States of America
New Directions books are printed on acid-free paper
First published clothbound and as New Directions Paperbook 648 in 1987
Published simultaneously in Canada by Penguin Books Canada Limited

Library of Congress Cataloging-in-Publication Data

Baca, Jimmy Santiago, 1952–
    Martín & Meditations on the South Valley.

        I. Baca, Jimmy Santiago, 1952–   Meditations on the South
Valley.   1987.   II. Title: Martín.   III.   Title: Meditations on
the South Valley.   IV.   Title: Martín and Meditations on the South
Valley.
PS3552.A254M37   1987   811'.54   87–10983
ISBN 0–8112–1031–6
ISBN 0–8112–1032–4 (pbk.)

Publisher's Note: Thanks are due to Tino Villanueva for his help with
the second printing.

New Directions Books are published for James Laughlin
by New Directions Publishing Corporation
80 Eighth Avenue, New York 10011

SIXTH PRINTING

FOR BEATRICE.

Please note: Throughout the poems phrases and passages of Chicano Spanish appear. A two-part glossary at the back of the book provides their English translations.

Contents

Introduction

Novels in verse, poetic autobiographies, epics—none of these genres is encountered very frequently, though perhaps each generation produces a few examples of the first two (the genuine epic is obviously far rarer) and there has been a distinct interest in narrative poetry in general in the last few years. Notable examples of the novel in verse to appear in recent years have been Vikram Seth's witty (and often moving) *The Golden Gate,* modeled on Pushkin's *Eugene Onegin,* and the English translation (by Randy Blasing and Mutlu Konuk) of Nazim Hikmet's *Human Landscapes,* that amazing work which borders on epic, and is more closely related to Kazantzakis's continuation of The Odyssey (and to its inspiration) than to Pushkin or, let's say, Crabbe. Jimmy Santiago Baca, in *Martín* and its sequel, *Meditations on the South Valley,* clearly has more affinity with Hikmet than with Seth's "new formalism." He draws directly upon personal and documentary material rather than on more distanced fictive constructions; and he writes with unconcealed passion: detachment is not a quality he cultivates. But he is far from being a naïve realist; what makes his work so exciting to me is the way in which it manifests both an intense lyricism and that transformative vision which perceives the mythic and archetypal significance of life-events.

The story told in *Martín* draws upon elements of Baca's own history, but does not duplicate them. Fictive names are employed, events telescoped, and whole epochs of experience eliminated, so that the core significance not be obscured or cluttered. The tale may be outlined: A boy abandoned by his parents lives first with a grandmother, then is placed in an orphanage. Relatives from both sides—the rural poor ones and the town bourgeois—take him out to visit occasionally. At ten he runs away. He lives from hand to mouth and becomes, outwardly, just another example of that familiar figure, a young man with "nothing to do, nowhere to go," hanging out on the corner of any Main Street— often a Black, Native American or Hispanic, and in this case a mestizo, Mejicano, "detribalized Apache." But Martín has the mind of a poet (and the reader—though not deliberately—is challenged: next time you see such a figure, remember that though his head *may* be filled only with quotidian banalities and with crude and trivial wishes, it is also very possible that he is living an inner life at least as vivid as your own). His imagination is engaged; in poverty, and witness to much brutality and degradation, he retains an innocent eye—a wild creature's eye—and a deep and loving respect for the earth. As a child he had dreamed an Indian spirit-dream, and sung "all earth is holy" over and over to his heart's drum beat. The street-wise youth holds secretly to that wisdom.

After some personal disasters he takes to the road and for some years wanders from state to state. While he is far from home the need to seek out his origins, to know his parents' stories, becomes strong in him. He calls to mind those who had known them, is haunted by their voices telling him of the tragic lives from which he sprang. He returns, and explores those lives, and experiences their bitter deaths.

Then Martín again goes wandering, from state to state, city to city: searching now for a point of rest, dreaming of a bit of land, and a house, and a woman who will be his wife. He searches, searches, in and out of trouble, discontented, broke, "thin with addiction," drifting. At last he is drawn back once more to "Burque," to his own New Mexican reality, and at last finds the woman he has dreamed of.

To make a home for her and himself and their coming child he guts and rebuilds an old shack and clears decades of scrap from the half-acre of land behind it. At the poem's end he has received the newborn into his own hands and sworn to his son that he will never abandon him.

Reduced to outline, it is a simple story, with barely a "plot." But in its poetic richness it is so much more—a Hero Tale, an archetypal journey, not only through a personal desolation but into, and out of, the desolated, benighted lives of his parents. Passing through the desert he emerges into a green and fertile valley of love and birth, but he has learned that the valley will be his to keep only if he cherishes it. The vow never to abandon his child as he had been abandoned (and as his father had abandoned *himself*—to drink; or as his mother had been essentially abandoned by *her* father, who exchanged responsible fatherhood for incestuous rape) extends beyond the child to "all living things." And this of necessity includes Martín's self; the vow implies that he will respect the holiness of his own life too, henceforth. Thus the poem is essentially a myth of redemption.

The second half of this volume, *Meditations on the South Valley,* can be recognized a sequel to *Martín* even though it is told in the first, not the third, person; but it is also an autonomous self-contained work. And within its totality, which forms a narrative, its parts can each be read as discrete entities, some of them meditative lyrics such as XVII or XIII for example, some of them stories within the framing story.

The *myth recognized in reality* in this poem is parallel to that told in *Martín. Meditations* opens with the destruction by fire of the hard-won house, the secure locus, the nest whose construction, along with the birth of a child, brought *Martín* to completion. The fire necessitates a period of residence in a neighborhood whose alien character, combined with the shock of that disaster, impels the writer to take stock of all that his own South Valley signifies to him: the warmth, passion, tragedy, *reality* of the barrio thrown into sharp relief by the suburban blandness of "the Heights." The resulting poems portray and evoke the values embodied in the barrio, despite—and in certain ways even because of—all its poverty and racial oppression. Cherished *old* things mended to serve anew are perceived in their beauty, compared to the glare and glitz of things shiny with newness.

> "Ah, those lovely bricks
> and sticks I found in fields
> and took home with me
> to make flower boxes!
> The old cars I've worked on
> endlessly giving them tune-ups,
> changing tires, tracing
> electrical shorts . . .
> . . . the process of making-do,
> of the life I've lived between
> breakdowns and break-ups . . .

I could not bear a life
with everything perfect."

In contrast, the rented "Heights" apartment "reflects a faceless person
. . . an emptiness" with its "white walls/thin orange carpet" all
"strangely clean and new" where there are no homely chores for him
to do. On the groomed suburban street people with "ceramic faces"
are walking their elegant clipped poodles, and "the air is blistered with
glaze/of new cars and new homes." As he longs for the barrio, an
organic *neighborhood,* he tells stories of its people, stories at once
typical and unique: "bad little Eddie," who cried out against injustice,
cared for his old grandmother, was illiterate, generous, a delinquent
piece of rubbish in the eyes of society, and died playing "chicken";
Pablo the powerful gang-leader, now a janitor, "still proud," still "cool
to the bone," who leads "a new gang of neighborhood parents" to fight
against water pollution; Feliz the *curandera,* who bewitches Caspar the
Ghost, who used to pick fights all the time and now stands on the Río
Grande bridge each day muttering religious curses, his shack papered
with images of the Sacred Heart; María the young witch; Pancho "the
barrio idiot," who identifies with the animals and lives his harmless life,
rich with fantasies, unmolested; Benny whom the Río Grande takes to
itself. . . . All these are seen within the society of which they are a
part, and thus the autonomy of each story, each poem within the poem
(including those which are most lyrical and personal) is never detached
from that wholeness of view which results from an artist's dedicated
engagement with experience.

Social criticism is implicit, not abstracted, throughout Baca's work—
most obviously in the prison poems of an earlier volume, *Immigrants
in Our Own Land,* though even there not divorced from a prevailing
lyricism. In the present book it is felt as the underlying theme: the trag-
edy of waste, deprivation, disinheritance. The illiterate youths "lean[ing]
on haunches in the sun/back[s] against a wall," "entangled in the rusty
barbed wire of a society [they] do not understand" are brothers and
comrades of Martín/Baca. He is aware, with Blakean vision, studying
"the faces of boys/playing in dirt yards," of Cuauhtémoc; in men who,
"eyes sleek with dreams,/lounge on porches/reading the flight of geese/
above the Río Grande," he perceives Netzahualcóyotl. But all of this

could not engage one, the reader could not really hear and feel it, if Baca's language itself did not engage the ear. It is not only his responsive sensibility that, at the very opening of *Martín,* enters presences that linger in the air of an abandoned pueblo like the former presence of a picture on a wall; it is the donative articulation with which he can transmit experience. How rich the spare, mostly monosyllabic cadences can be! He evokes his childhood:

> "On *that* field
> I hand swept smooth
> top crust dirt and duned a fort.
> Idling sounds of Villa's horse
> I reared my body and neighed at weeds."

Or the childhood of his mother, after the school bus has dropped her off at the edge of the field track she must follow home:

> "The lonely aftrenoon in the vast expanse of llano
> was a blue knife
> sharpening its hot, silver edge on the distant
> horizon of mountains, the wind blew over
> chipping red grit, carving a prehistoric scar-scaled
> winged reptile of the mountain. . . ."

His imagery often has the Gongoresque character (which in Neruda is called "surreal" but has little to do with cerebral French-style surrealism) common to much Hispanic writing (traceable, perhaps, to Arabic influences in Spain, and to Native American influences in the New World?). Such images surprise, but are rooted in actual observation. "Laughter rough as brocaded cloth . . . teeth brilliant as church tiles"—the comparisons are fresh and real, and give a kind of beauty to the roughness, a dignity to the sensual gleam of teeth.

The young, homeless Martín makes friends with old women who hang out by the bars, "blue teardrops tattooed on their cheeks,/initials of ex-lovers on their hands." They are perceived as

> "drawn out from the dark piss-stinking rooms
> they lived in,

                    by the powerful force of the moon,
                    whose yellow teeth tore the alfalfa out of their hearts
                    and left them stubbled,
                    parched grounds old goats of Tecatos and winos
                    nibbled"

—a metaphor that beautifully balances both its terms; they have equal, virtually interchangeable validity.

By the time we return, in the *Meditations,* to the narrator's own story, the containing frame, we can perceive that what makes it so imperative to rebuild the burned house is not only the obvious practical and psychological need anyone, anywhere, might have after a fire, but the need once more to reenter the history and struggle of his own people.

The actual reconstruction (aided by friends whose character, once again, might seem highly dubious to the world at large, but who, in solidarity, rise to the occasion with honor) is a miniature epic, Homeric in its condensed enumeration of the details the herculean labor involved.

The felling of an ancient elm which precedes the clearing of the house-site before the building begins is a particularly powerful passage, which once more demonstrates Baca's unforced feeling for symbolic significance. The death of the great elephantine tree is a necessary ritual of mythic character; the author, although now "where the tree had stood/a silver waterfall of sky poured down," feels as if he had "just killed an old man." But myth is entered through the graphic, sonic, and kinesthetic evocation of an actual, strenuous event, in which human effort and the last "leaf-heave" breath of a shuddering, cracking, down-crashing tree become part of the reader's own experience.

At last the work of construction is done, and a new house much better than the first has come into being. It is a birth, to parallel the birth of the little son in *Martín.* Ten years of poems had been burned in the fire—new ones are born in meditation and action. Not the house nor the poems only, and not even the return to the South Valley and what it symbolizes, but—parallel to the vow of commitment at the end of *Martín*—new levels of awareness, dedication, purpose, and personal freedom, emerge as phoenix from these ashes.

                                                     Denise Levertov

Martín

I

Pinos Wells—
an abandoned pueblo now.
The presence of those who lived
in these crumbling adobes
lingers in the air
like a picture
removed
leaves its former presence on the wall.

In corral dust
medicinal bottles
preserve rusty sunshine
that parched this pueblo
30 years ago.
Blackened sheds rust
in diablito barbs.
In barn rafters cobwebs
hang intricate as tablecloths
grandma crocheted for parlors
of wealthy Estancia ranchers.
Now she spins silken spider eggs.

My mind circles warm ashes of memories,
the dark edged images of my history.
On *that* field
I hand swept smooth
top crust dirt and duned a fort.

Idling sounds of Villa's horse
I reared my body and neighed at weeds.

From the orphanage my tía Jenny
drove me to Pinos Wells
to visit grandma. All Saturday afternoon
her gnarled fingers
flipped open photo album pages
like stage curtains at curtain call
the strange actors of my mestizo familia
bowed before me wearing vaquero costumes,
mechanic overalls and holding hoes in fields.

At the six o'clock mass
with clasped hands I whispered
to the blood shackled Christ on the cross,
begging company with my past—
given to Christ who would never tell
how under the afternoon sun in Santa Fe
the rooster slept and black ants
formed rosaries over the hard dirt yard,
when . . .

                Sanjo barrio,

                            Chucos parked

at Lionel's hamburger stand
to watch Las Baby Dolls
cruise Central avenue,
chromed excitement of '57 Chevies
flashing in their eyes.

In the alley behind Jack's Package Liquors
dogs fight for a burrito
dropped from a wino's coat pocket.
The ambulance screams down Edith
into Sanjo where Felipe bleeds red whiskey
through knife wounds.

On Walter street
telephones ring in red-stone apartments
while across Broadway
under Guadalupe bridge
box-car gypsies and Mejicanos swig Tokay.
Corridos—
  chairs splintering on kitchen floors—
  arguing voices in dark porches—
   doors angrily slammed—
    Seagrams bottles shatter on the street—

I fell
into Sanjo, into my own brown body,
not knowing how to swim
as tongues lashed white spray warning
of storms to come,
             I prayed.

In Santa Fe as a boy
I watched red tractors crumble dirt,
the black fire of disc blades
upturning burned leaves and cornstalks in their wake,
while I collected green and red commas
of broken glass in my yard,
and romped in mud slop of fallen tomb-trunks
of cottonwoods
that steamed in the dawn by the ditch.
Then,
        the fairytale of my small life
          stopped
when mother and father
abandoned me, and the ancient hillgods of my emotions
in caves of my senses
screamed, and the corn seedling of my heart
withered—like an earth worm out of earth,
I came forth into the dark world of freedom.

I ran from the orphanage at ten,
worked at Roger's Sheet Metal shop.
I'd open the window to let morning breeze
cool my boy body, and shoo
sparrows from their window ledge nest.

At the Conquistador Inn on south Central
I made love to Lolita,
and after her father found out, Lolita
slashed her wrists,
sitting on the toilet, blood scribbling
across the yellow linoleum,
as her brother pushed me aside, lifted her,
and drove her away, I nodded goodbye.

Teenage years
I sought that dark connection
of words become actions, of dreams made real,
like Tijerina's courthouse raid,
of César Chávez and thousands of braceros
enduring the bloody stubs of police batons
that beat them as they marched.

I ransacked downtown stores
for winter coats to give my friends,
and the National Guard gassed me
at the Roosevelt Park when we burned
a cop's car to the ground.
He clubbed a Chicana for talking back.

On the West Mesa,
I took long walks and listened for a song
to come to me, song of a better life,
while an old Navajo woman sat on her crate
and groaned wet lipped at the empty wine bottle,
in front of Louie's Market

and gummy drunks staggered to sun by the wall,
mumbling moans for money.

Vatos in Barelas
leaned into their peacoats
against winter wind, faces tempered
with scars, as they rattled down pebbly alleys
to their connection's house.

At the University of New Mexico
learned Chicanos
lugged book-heavy ideas to bed
and leafed through them sleeplessly,
while I slept under cottonwood trees
along the Río Grande
and cruised with Pedro
drinking whiskey through the Sangre de Cristo
mountains, until we hurled off
a sharp snowy curve one December morning
into a canyon, and I carried his dead body to a farm house.

Months after I headed West
on I-40,
in my battered Karmen Ghia.
Desperate for a new start,
sundown in my face,
I spoke with Earth—

> I have been lost from you Mother Earth.
> No longer
> does your language of rain wear away my thoughts,
> nor your language of fresh morning air
> wear away my face,
> nor your language of roots and blossoms
> wear away my bones.
> But when I return, I will become your child again,

let your green alfalfa hands take me,
let your maiz roots plunge into me
and give myself to you again,
with the crane, the elm tree and the sun.

*   *   *   *

II

I gave myself to the highway
like a bellrope in the wind
searching for a hand.

In Arizona,
fieldworkers' porchlights
shimmered turquoise
in the distant cardboard farm towns.

The highway was a black seed split
petals of darkness blossomed from,
black matted hair of night rain
hung down over.

Everything hoped for in my life
was a rock closed road,
where I had left my identity,
                and my family.

Nights turn into days
with the steady swath of a mason's trowel,
and silence sticks to my heart like dried mortar.
I imagine my man-hand
will build a good life,
and through the miles I dream myself
a different man,

                sprung from the innocent child
                in Corrales, picking apples
                under aging branches, I tug
                and shake, as apples crunch through the air
                onto the tractor matted grass.
                I shoulder my gunny sack to the truck
                and Don Carlos heaves it up, appling
                on apples.

Catholic holidays
Franciscan nuns bussed us
to Jémez mountain parks.
The old yellow bus gagged
round tree tangled curves
and looming walls of stone,
canyon depths flashed mesquite
enfolding green hills between green hills,
until at the mountaintop, I summed
layers and layers of distant dustland drift,
as the bus gear grudged and nuns nagged
us to sing prayers, until we jolted
down a dirt road to the sunny picnic grounds.

* * * *

III

For some years I wandered cross country,
and those who had known my parents
came back to me again.

On a fallen oak, limbs in pond,
sat old one-armed Pepín—
"Martín, your father and I
were in the El Fidel cantina
with unas viejas one afternoon.
Tú sabes, nos pusimos bien chatos.
And then Sheri, your mamá, walks in.
I don't remember what she asked Danny,
but la vieja with your father said,
I thought your wife was crippled.
Sheri started crying and sin una palabra,
turned and went out."

The religious voice of blind Estela Gómez
blackened the air one day.
"92 years mijito. ¿Qué pasó? There were no more
beans to pick, no crops to load on trains.
Pinos Wells dried up, como mis manos.
Everyone moved away to work. I went to Estancia,
con mi hijo Reynaldo.
Gabachos de Tejas, we worked for them. Loading
alfalfa, picking cotton for fifty cents a row.
¿Y Danny? La borrachera. ¿Y Sheri? La envidia.
That's what happened, Martín, to your familia."

Wrapped in her sarape, Señora Martínez
hunched toward me in the falling snow flakes.
"Sheri was scared to go home for her purse,

so she sent me. Dios mío, I'll never forget that day,
mijo. When I opened the closet door, there was Danny,
standing with a butcher knife raised high,
ready to kill."

I heard Merlinda Griego's voice
coming from the creek. It was soft
as a leaf spinning in creek current.
"You cried a lot Martín. Dios mío cómo llorabas.
A veces your jefito brought you to Las Flores cantina
where I waitressed. He came to see me. You played
on the floor with empty whiskey miniatures.
We were at El Parque cooling our feet in the water,
when your mother came up to me, screamed
that I gave you mal ojo. I thought she was going to drown me.
Quién sabe mijo, all I remember
is that she was jealous."

Month after month I heard the voices.
Pancho Garza, Piggly Wiggly manager in Santa Fe,
"I gave her bruised fruit and crumbled cookie packages,
sometimes a sack of flour. Danny drank up her paycheck.
Besides, she was a good checker."

From behind a red house at the edge of woods,
Antonia Sánchez, la bruja de Torreón,
called out,
"¿Dónde está tu mamá? Safe from that madman.
Se casó otra vez y tiene dos niños. No,
no te puedo decir dónde viven."

I took red dried mud paths
bordered with sultry harvest crops and woods.
Bending under briar riggings, blue worm bait dangling

down deer trails, as I skipped
creek rocks, straddled sagged fences,
'til I found a secluded pond,
bullrush choked, I thrashed to the shore,
tossed my line out
big-mouth bass puckered water rings by,
as the nylon line rippled slowly down
on the water. I fished
'til I could no longer see my bait
plop, 'til the far shore disappeared and the moon
bobbed on the black water
a candle flame in a window in the darkness.

On my back in the grass, looking at the stars,
I said aloud to myself,
I'm leaving in the morning.

Days later in the Texas panhandle
harvest dust smolders and insects whiff
empty crates and vegetable boxes
stacked against produce stands.
Wings of bees wedge board bin cracks
sticky with chile mash, and flies gorge
in tin pails and buzz in paper sacks
dropped on the sawdusted earthen floor.
Alongside the stand, rugged eight wheelers
glazed with potato guck, simmer hot rubber
and grease odors, side-board racks oozing with crushed fruits.

Your departure uprooted me mother,
hollowed core of child
your absence whittled down
to a broken doll
in a barn loft. The small burned area of memory,
where your face is supposed to be,
moons' rings pass through

in broken chain of events
in my dreams.

* * * *

IV

Grandma Lucero at the table
smokes Prince Albert cigarette
rolled from a can,
sips black coffee from metal cup,
and absorbs hours of silence
like prairie sky absorbs campfire smoke.
Death hangs over her shoulders
a black cow's hide
slung over the fence to dry.
She had once been a brimming acequia
her four sons drank from
like bighorn sheep.

Conversations in her kitchen
about my mother I overheard as a boy,
made me sniff around the screen door to hear more,
like a coyote smells a cave he had been born in once.
My animal eyes and skin
twitched with fear. I created myself in a field,
beside the house, where lizard and rabbit
breathed in my ear
stories of eagles and arrowheads. My heart
became an arroyo, and my tears cut deep cracks
in my face of sand, when tía Jenny came to take me away
from grandma. With rocks in my pockets
earth had bit off for me like soft bread
for the long journey,
I left Estancia for the orphanage.

As we drove through Tijeras mountains,
I looked back,
distant fields grooved with hoofpaths
of grazing cattle and sheep.
Grandma's knee-length gray hair,

she brushed and brushed every morning,
braided, bunned, and wrapped
with a black tápalo.
Long gray rain clouds hung over
the crumbling train-track town—
then lightning crackled
like the slap of new lumber stacks,
and rain darkened
the plaster cracks of grandma's adobe house.

I had an image of mother in the morning
dancing in front of the mirror
in pink panties,
masking her face with mascara,
squeezing into tight jeans.
Her laughter rough as brocaded cloth
and her teeth brilliant as church tiles.

On visiting days with aunts and uncles,
I was shuttled back and forth—
between Chávez bourgeois in the city
and rural Lucero sheepherders,
new cars and gleaming furniture
and leather saddles and burlap sacks,
noon football games and six packs of cokes
and hoes, welfare cards and bottles of goat milk.

I was caught in the middle—
between white skinned, English speaking altar boy
at the communion railing,
and brown skinned, Spanish speaking plains nomadic child
with buffalo heart groaning underworld earth powers,
between Sunday brunch at a restaurant
and burritos eaten in a tin-roofed barn,
between John Wayne on the afternoon movie
rifle butting young Braves,
and the Apache whose red dripping arrow

was the altar candle in praise of the buck
just killed.

Caught between Indio-Mejicano rural uncles
who stacked hundred pound sacks of pinto beans
on boxcars all day, and worked the railroad tracks
behind the Sturgis sheds, who sang Apache songs
with accordions, and Chávez uncles and aunts
who vacationed and followed the Hollywood model
of My Three Sons for their own families,
sweeping the kitchen before anyone came to visit,
looking at photo albums in the parlor.

When I stayed with the Chávezes
I snuck out of the house, wandered at will,
heading south to the ditches of the South Valley,
and when they caught up with me days later,
I smelled of piñón bark
from wood piles I had played on,
and the red brown clay stuck to my shoes
from corrals I had entered to pet a horse,
smeared over the new interior car carpet.
They stopped inviting me out.

On my cot one night at the orphanage,
I dreamed my spirit was straw and mud,
a pit dug down below my flesh
to pray in,
and I prayed on beads of blue corn kernels,
slipped from thumb to earth,
while deerskinned drumhead of my heart
gently pounded and I sang

> all earth is holy,
> all earth is holy,
> all earth is holy,
> all earth is holy,

until a nun shook me awake.

Next day I ran away,
and drifted barrios of Burque,
stealing food from grocery stores,
sleeping in churches, and every dark dawn,
walking and walking and walking,
my eyes shaded with fear and my life
dimmed to a small shadow—
an old coal mine shaft
that kept falling in on me,
burying me in black sands of a murky past.

* * * *

V

Years pass.
Cattle cars in the downtown freightyard
squeal and groan, and sizzling grills
steam the Barelas Coffee House cafe windows,
as the railroad workers with tin hard hats
stop for coffee, hours of dawn
softly click on grandfathers' gold pocket watches
in Louey's Broadway Pawnshop, hocked
to get a cousin or brother out of jail.
City workers' tin carts and long-handled dust pans
clatter in curb gutters
as buses spew smoldering exhaust as they stop beneath
Walgreen's neon liquor sign.
I lean against an office building brick wall,
nothing to do, no where to go,
comb my hair in the blue tinted office windows,
see my reflection in the glinting chromed cars,
on a corner, beneath a smoking red traffic light,
I live—
          blue beanie cap snug over my ears
                    down to my brow,
in wide bottomed jean pants trimmed with red braid,
I start my daily walk,
                    to the Old Town Post Office,
                    condemned Armijo school building,
                    Río Grande playa,
                    ditches and underpasses—
de-tribalized Apache
entangled in the rusty barbwire of a society I do not understand,
Mejicano blood in me spattering like runoff water
from a roof canale, glistening over the lives
who lived before me, like rain over mounds of broken pottery,
each day backfills with brown dirt of my dreams.

I lived in the streets,
slept at friends' houses, spooned
pozole and wiped up the last frijoles with tortilla
from my plate. Each day
my hands hurt for something to have,
and a voice in me yearned to sing,
and my body wanted to shed the gray skin of streets,
like a snake that grew wings—
I wished I had had a chance to be a little boy,
and wished a girl had loved me,
and wished I had had a family—but these
were silver inlaid pieces of another man's life,
whose destiny fountained over stones and ivy
of the courtyard in a fairytale.

Each night I could hear the silver whittling blade
of La Llorona,
carving a small child on the muddy river bottom,
like a little angel carved into ancient church doors.
On Fridays, Jesus Christ appeared
on La Vega road, mounted on a white charger,
his black robe flapping in the moonlight
as he thrashed through bosque brush.
Sometimes Wallei, the voice of water, sang to me,
and Mectallá, who lives in the fire, flew in the air,
and Cuzal, the Reader of Rocks, spoke with a voice
jagged as my street-fighting knuckles.

A voice in me soft as linen
unfolded on midnight air,
to wipe my loneliness away—the voice blew open
like a white handkerchief in the night
embroidered with red roses,
waving and waving from a dark window
at some lover who never returned.

I became a friend of the old women
who hung out by the bars
on Central,
    Broadway,
    Isleta,
    and Barcelona,
blue tear drops tattooed on their cheeks,
initials of ex-lovers on their hands,
women drawn out from the dark piss-stinking rooms
they lived in,
by the powerful force of the moon,
whose yellow teeth tore the alfalfa out of their hearts,
and left them stubbled,
parched grounds old goats of tecatos and winos
nibbled.

All my life the constant sound of someone's bootheels
trail behind me—thin, hard,
sharp sounds scraping frozen ground,
like a shovel digging a grave.
It's my guardian, following me through the broken branches
of the bosque, to the door
of the Good Shepherd Home on south 2nd. street,
for a hot meal.

*   *   *   *

VI

At dawn
rusted field iron
stocks tanks and gates smolder mist.
Engine echoes hum in deep shafts of grey dawn silence,
then whirr away beyond the railroad tracks.

Padre Padilla
tugs the knotted bell rope, claps the iron
welcome to black veiled viejas
mumbling Spanish prayers
as they walk
down field paths
meandering to the church.
Some men arrive on horses
shuddering dew from their flanks,
and snorting at the sweet scent of field flowers.

Distant groans from St. Francis church
reach you mother
as you scrape seed out
of the feed sack, slop last night's supper
greens to chickens,
and pail windmill water to calves and pigs.

You were the most beautiful girl in the pueblo,
good natured, smiling, green eyed and white skinned.
After school the bus left you
on tracks you followed home.
The lonely afternoon in the vast expanse of llano,
was a blue knife
sharpening its hot, silver edge on the distant
horizon of mountains, the wind blew over
chipping red grit, carving a pre-historic scar-scaled
winged reptile of the mountain,

that breathed a cool sigh at dusk,
whirling sand at your ankles,
rustling cornstalks and rippling water in troughs,
blowing your thick flowing hair.

You hung out at the local gas station,
dreamed of being a calendar pin-up girl,
and for hours flipped
through romance magazines, and imagined yourself
in a bathing suit,
embraced by a matinee idol.

At 13, your
father climbed the steps
to your room, and his fingers
stroked between your thighs and warmed
your blood. Outside,
the leaf skinned snake
slithered in arroyo silt grain
to warm itself
in the stored sun's heat.

For two years
your father drew his dull life
like a knife from a sheath
and found happiness in the wound.
You vowed
never to be vulnerable again
after you left home.

In the painful afterglow of sex,
after he left your room,
you stayed awake
learning cunning from coyotes
that prowled scrap-wood corrals,
learning endurance
from the windmill's grunting pipe

and creaking fan blades,
and you dreamed in the darkness
the night train
that snaked across the prairie,
pulled you onto its rattling boxcars
toward California.

While he read scripture one evening
from his black Bible,
you told him
you were carrying a backseat baby—
                his calloused hands
                gripped the wooden arm chair rests,
                his haggard face whitened,
                and his silence carved
                stone doors in the air,
                you walked through,
                slowly closing the door on him.

Cruising out of Willard
with Danny, in a new black Ford,
your heart gave its first wingspread,
and soared in your body
that now felt like a nest.
You thought of me
planted in the soft furrow of your body,
and knew I would become
field prey.

A few days after I was born,
you filed for divorce,
left me at grandma's door
and ran away to California
with your lover.

This act of abandonment
was God's will,

and it left no scent, no view, no mark
others might find.
My image of you
fell into my life, across my life
like a massive black branch
sparkling with snow frost,
that filled the air with a vast space of lights,
softly glowing in the darkness.

I was never told
where you were at,
and not until your return years later,
when I was man,
did the snow crust melt
and your hands drift up like yellow flowers
I plucked,
and your face float by like a mask
I wore.

Time had spun a white veil
around the dream you were,
and now your words were moths
eating through the white veil,
as you told me of the frayed-skirt life
father had given you.

Each day of your absence
had become aged stone between us,
unbudged for decades. Now in the ruins,
the chill scream of a baby
came to us from a distant adobe shack,
and drowned our voices out.

We never spoke with each other again,
until several years after our meeting,
a telephone call came around midnight.

"Your mother has been shot,
and she won't make it through the night."

Swollen mass of bruised flesh,
mangled half-face inhuman thing
tubed and monitored on the bed,
wrapped in gauzes soaked in blood.

"Unplug the machine," I told the doctor.

Polishing her nails
in the kitchen, her husband
fired four shots
into her beautiful face,
because he felt she was going to leave him,
because she would no longer
live in his make-believe world.

Each bullet opened another door of her life,
to interminable darkness,
she walked in,
over meat scraps and bone fragments,
into her own being,
deeper, until the bullets sounded like a boutique
shop doorbell, hurling her past
shelves of rock-slag scrub-brush farmland
she grew up on, into the warm arms
of a woman rocking her by a fireplace,
where she closed her eyes and slept.

I found her diary
lying on her dresser,
and read it.

"I want to die,
I have no one in this world,
I want to die,"

written
hundreds of times.
Her daughter, my stepsister, rushed in,
ripped the diary from my hands,
and burned it in the fireplace.
I had already read
how the family had lived
months without talking to each other,
how mother had spiraled into love affairs
with young men
her daughter had been in love with,
how mother wanted to destroy a marriage,
and find someone who could give her
one kind word, one small gift of concern
and appreciation.

On the refrigerator,
written in lipstick, he scrawled,

> "You will never leave me!
> You will never go out
> on me again!"

Then he took his own life.

A long time ago
he thought he had saved you,
from your own culture, your own language,
and drove you from the dust and tumbleweeds of Santa Fe,
across the llano,
to grassy valleys of California.

He placed your photograph
on his fireplace mantle,
a trophy of a young girl
saved from her own people.
He thought of life as a Wild West film,
and himself a quiet, resourceful cowboy.

When you pulled the plug
on the tv,
when you seized your destiny again,
shattered his trophy,
lonely and desolate night poured through the windows
of your house,
the misery of dim street lamps
lit your faces,
and you realized you were both old,
you both had been living a false dream,
and your throats coughed with sickness,
and your voices strained with the tragedy
that you had lived a fairytale—

Then he shot you and himself.

*   *   *   *

VII

All that remain
are the names
on baptismal records
in the Tomé church—
Micaela,
      Telesfora,
            Román y José.

Whatever else
may tell me
where I come from,
crackles in claws
of horny toads
in rock niches,
or is shredded by a hawk
for its nest.

Father,
set adrift in darkness,
no tribal magnetic field
to point the way,
you lost your bearing,
your direction home,
and became trapped
in a motel room.

I first saw you
on a bright Sunday morning,
on North 4th street,
under canopy shade of the used-car
sales office, reclined
in a folding chair,
paper spread in open arms.

In the wellshaft
of your sunglasses' gleaming black water,
a small boy dreamed
of a father—
over the black water, as you looked at me,
light glinted away the darkness
of tomorrow,
and to be near you blinded me.

The visit ended,
and the flickering wick
of your words,
that guided me down
into the white center of a dawn,

now blackened and smoldered
over my legs dangling
from the doorless
backend of a bus,
that shook down field roads
to the orphange,
past corn and bean rows
I hoed.

Time of day, time of year,
and holidays,
broke down
after our visit,
you numbed yourself to me
with a jug of healing whiskey,
'til I was a blur of pain
trailing you
to backroom poker games,
faded downtown
pool halls
and musty bars.

Like a plant with its tendency
to move toward the light, I survived,
warmed myself around
fuel drum
next to padlocked gates at the railroad.
On cold nights—
windowpanes
swathed in frost,
while wind clattered
thin bones of picket fences,
and cracked gray haired ice
clinging to eaves,
I rubbed my hands
close to barrel flames
and remembered—

Times you scared me,
turned up your eyelids
to pink hoods,
raised your arms monster
walking toward me
as I crouched in fear.

Or while
stray dogs' breath
spewed steam,
and they snarled in clotted food wrappers,
and police sirens
cleaved the night sky, inside
a small apartment
some where,
you took your shirt off
and let me scratch your back.

One night I have never forgotten—
staggering out of the A-1 bar
into the alley,

you saw me,
approached, lipping a saliva soaked butt,
and cuffed me, cursed me,
cuffed me again,
growling no good   no good
between swigs of whiskey.

I had never raised my hand against anyone.
Then anger entwined
through the long plait of my black hair,
crown of thorns
circles and dots tattooed
on my brown hide breast,
became symbols of rebellion,
as black mass of fury
held out its smoking hands
over my eyes,
and I kicked you down
vomiting whiskey
to the ground.

Then I fled
into the night,
crucifix and scapulary
swinging out of my shirt, I ran
into brown boundaries
of Barelas barrio,
wind had caved in elm branches
in yards like old cemetery crosses,
amidst which I mourned
death of my respect
for you.

I never saw you again father.
But you stayed with me,
a fragile altar piece,
arms broken off,

leg cracked,
I kept trying to repair
to its original state.

You left Burque
so others wouldn't see you
a vagrant drunk, and rented a room
in Frisco,
with mildewy ceilings and rotted floorboards,
mattress matted and with dried sweat and blood,
stained with semen,
on which you lay
clutching your body seized with pain
after drinking three fifths of Seagrams.

On the wooden cart of your bones,
you rode,
on your way to the gallows,
wrists and ankles tied with black strips of terror,
mouth gagged with a shriek—
figure of pain
in the dark cellar of your room,
awaiting death,
you raved vague remedies
and promises,
and by morning limped in your undershorts
about the room, bleary eyed,
mumbling to yourself,
checking your pants pockets for coins
to buy yourself a cup of poison.

You wrote me a letter
from the de-tox center—

        My son Martín—
                I will be leaving the hospital
                tomorrow. I have been sick. I will

send you some money to come see me.
Maybe you will stay for awhile with me.

    love,

    your father

Two days after he left the de-tox center,
a policeman found him
in the gutter. In his overcoat pocket
stuck to the ice, they found the letter.

Your life
father was a prolonged death,
gambling lands and house away,
submerging your feelings
for forty years
like embryos in whiskey bottles,
afraid to let them cry, to breathe,
to curse and praise life.

Grandma lit a candle
next to your picture
on the church altar,
and at your headstone
placed a paper flower
on a wire stem
to shade you from the sun,
like her rebozo
when you were a baby
shaded you from the sun.

At the funeral
mother placed a rose
in the coffin
on your folded hands.
I see your finger bones

a throne
you hoist the rose on
like a small sacred statue
you march
beneath the earth
in your private feast day.

Where ever I am at
and I happen to think of you,
cool breeze
hums an old Apache song
deep in its throat
and sings my pain to peace.

But there is no reprieve
from the pain
from not having embraced each other,
just once,
from not having talked with each other,
just once.

* * * *

VIII

After my parents' death
I left Burque again, to buy a house,
a small piece of land,
and marry a woman. I lost myself
in the swarm-noise of big cities,
rain-gutted sideroads
aromatic with field flowers,
and lived with women
in the woods, their unattended children
playing in broken pick-ups in the yard,
while old mothers
sat on the porch, the odor
of rubbing alcohol
on their arthritic legs
filled my nostrils.

On the outskirts of Dallas,
in Ohio, Michigan and Louisiana,
in countless towns,
long haired and bearded, wearing jeans and plaid shirt,
in scruffed workboots,

I skimmed each face,
like a missing stone
looking for its mask,
innocent as a shattered quartz
under the sledge of chance and luck.

Each city was filled
with children
like the child I had once been
who learned pain of a match that burned a thumb,
a fire-cracker that exploded in a tiny palm,
who sat in an ant pile
until the tiny body speckled with stings,
who learned to be a hero early

and sleep out in the fold-out couch
in an aunt's livingroom,
and who dozed off to bedtime stories
of dogs and frogs on ditchbanks,
who sang of a world somewhere
for children,
where they would have their own rooms,
toys, new shoes, and ice creams on hot summer noons.

And like these children,
welfare checks that came for me
aunt spent on tires and cigarettes
for my cousin. These children
learned to roll their shirt cuffs up,
pomade hair back into a ducktail,
toss the white dice of their heart and soul
onto mean street curbs,
hoping each roll
would make a dream come true.

There were children like me
all across the world. In the yellowed pages
of afternoons, while back-yard trash smoldered in barrels,
and greasy motors hanging on welded tripod pipes
dripped oil and penned black letters
on driveway cement,
                    about Johnny who married,
                    Lorenzo killed in Nam,
                    Eddie en la Pinta,
                    Ramon who OD'd in Califas,
these children once with a dream,
now grown into adults, let their dream
dull against the iron hour-files
of minimum wage jobs,
emptied their dream
with each bottle of Tequila drained,

'til eventually it lost its cosmic luster
in casual one-night stands,
and faded into a naive, childhood wish,
a trading-post souvenir key-chain
given away as easily
as pocket change on gas and cigarettes.

I still had my dream for a better life,
and yearned for it,
like the Mesquite tree
in the desert
howls thirst
for lush storm runoffs.

So I returned to Burque.

*   *   *   *

Dawn in the Manzano mountains.
Pine and piñón from chimneys
smoke the curving road
with resinous mist.
My black feathered heart
effortlessly glides
in the clear blue sky
above the pueblos
de Manzano, Tajique, Willard y Estancia.
At the foothills
my grandmother herded sheep
and my grandfather planted corn y chile.

I turn my motorcycle off
next to QUARAI RUINS,
and silence drops
into the canyon

sounding an ancient song of sadness,
like a distant boulder
echoing into the blue sky and stubble grass.

I step into the open rock-pit
hollowed in earth
with flat rock door facing east,
pinch red clay and chew
my teeth black with earth prayer,
                    then speak with QUARAI—

O QUARAI! Shape
the grit and sediment I am,
mineral de Nuevo Mejico.

I will learn the dark red Apache words
and wind burnished chants,
the blazed red Spanish names of things
that absorb centuries of my blood.

Blow your lower-world breath
into my journey, O QUARAI!
I am ready to work,
all I ask is that I don't starve,
that I don't fail at being a good man,
that things go good for me,
that I meet a woman who will love me deeply,
that I meet strong spiritual brothers and sisters,
and that I have healthy children.

O QUARAI,
these things I promise—
to work hard and stay close to Mother Earth,
to raise my children through your eyes,
to teach them the old names of things,
and pray to the four directions.

I will not run
when You appear to me
as I did when younger, O QUARAI.
I will be strong and listen, and follow.

                    *   *   *   *

As I swerved back down mountain curves,
crunching rock chippings
from finished arrowheads, piñón nuts
and pine cones, the sun rose
and embered QUARAI monument with fiery light.

I thought I saw the dark-skinned ghost
of my grandfather, on his horse, with sombrero,
waving to me from QUARAI,
and the gray-haired ghost of my grandmother,
carding sheep fur
beneath the green teepee of a pine tree,
by the arroyo.

                    *   *   *   *

IX

In Burque,
rake teeth shine new with garden work,
and skinny girls pungent with dime-store perfume
walk splintered bleachers with scuffed barefeet,
giggling at unbranded studs
of footballs players at evening high school practice.
Fields and gardens exude rough passions
that despise hotel rooms and locked doors,
while the priest at St. Ann's church
stands on the steps before evening mass and smiles
a golden place in his smile
no one has found yet, where all the poor
will settle down in one day.

                    Ah Burque,
it is good to be back.
I take a job as night watchman on the city outskirts,
and during the night
listen to the gunned engine hum of diesels
on the interstate,
trucking pine logs to the nearby mill,
whose blades are frightened cats in the distance
snarling and whining at the moon rings in each log.
Across the dew glimmering black fields
odors of animal dung. The calm night air
flecked with insects
that pool around the porch light bulb.

                    *   *   *   *

Then I meet you Gabriela—
in your drafty, white-stucco frame house on Vassar,
we drink wine after supper

and tell stories—each hour
a wax candle that leads us back to a dark past,
away from each other and back again,
to the end of an empty green wine bottle,

                                        on the table,

at two a.m.

Tattered ends of months and years
now give us shelter and warmth—the crumbling shack
of my life white pigeons of dreams nested in,
now flew to give news of my life
to you.
Until morning we talked, until the white wing beat
of dawn folded its wings across our features,
and shaped a silence of love on them.

                    *   *   *   *

O, how long I looked for you Gabriela,
wandering lobbies, noon-time traffic,
narrow street cafes and roadside restaurants—
                        Blue bull day
urged me on, chrome vein pipes
of my cycle swollen,
foaming heat hill after hill, breathing rage hard
through city after city.
                    And at night,
I let my motorcycle cool to a cold blue beneath a tree,
and I'd stare at the paper lantern moon
swaying above black water night,
as white moths of stars slept,
                        I wondered
about my drifting nature,
what I was looking for, why so discontent. . . .
Then dawn opened her door,
and the long-haired, ragged and hungry world

awoke, and like a leaf I blew onward,
thin with addiction and busted broke.

                                    I looked for you
Gabriela,
even as I picked my clothing
from a motel room floor,
my lips raw-damp from another woman's kisses,
as I drove out of the parking lot,
burning headlight smoldered haze—
you were the mist,
always forming, always beyond grasp,
airy and fleeting.

Weary of the nightclub district,
I roamed Barelas
where blue flowers entwined rotting picket fences,
and in Sanjo, female voices behind screen doors
were as rich as brimming cups of dark wine,
and in the South Valley, women appeared
and receded on ditch paths, moon poised over them,
trying to catch them as they ran into tree clusters
or behind adobe houses.

In Central cafe windows
I saw glasses and plates, rumpled napkin
and magazine left open on the table,
and I wondered if it was you Gabriela
who had just eaten and left. . . .
                            Every sign
I took to mean you had been there,
a step ahead of me,
and as I turned, you turned, leaving
at my approach, where ever I went.

My motorcycle parked under a cottonwood,
in the bosque next to the river,

love ached in me as I watched geese
unfold white wings in the sky,
following the turgid flow of the river,
as I followed you,
the gleam of lap water over stones in the sand,
a porch light flicked on at night
to a stranger's knock on the door.

＊　＊　＊　＊

I moved in with you Gabriela—
house furnished with second-hand furniture,
frayed wicker rocking chair,
leaning book shelves, woolen wall-hangings,
wood and wool stitched blinds,
oak wood couch, and phone ringing constantly
you answered to console, comfort and talk with friends.

Our hearts were crag peaks of pottery
brown based with Autumn's falling leaves,
with a white stripe of first fallen snow—
our hearts were a fragment of our first winter love,
we buried in the earth of each other's palms.
Time passed,
and each day the six o'clock news
washed ashore debris of a wrecked world
far away from us.
I played my guitar and sang you songs,
tossing the words, *I love you,*
my life-savings, I had saved so long,
into the white foamy hours spent with you—
wave on wave into one wave
we came together, in high leaping brightness,
growing and weakening, flashing
in black evolutions of love,
as our battered memories and broken deposits of dreams,

scattered like seashells at our barefeet,
we picked up and blew our songs through.

*   *   *   *

One morning I passed our bedroom Gabriela,
glanced in at you, and wrote this poem—

Woman Lying In Bed

on Saturday morning.
Two dogs in the backyard
snoozing under shade tree.
The radio hums soft songs.
The earth is cool and watered,
sleepy eyed leaves hardly stir.
Sparrows peck food from the dog bowl.
She wonders on her life.
She has a book in her hand
and in another room
the stereo coos love songs.
Her naked body: leg crooked up,
the other stretched out;
sheets tousled to the side.
She thinks: life is good
with this man.
She turns the pages of the book
absentminded and the window
to her left
fans her body with cool breeze.
She is woman
carrying a child.
It purrs.
Life has been delayed.
For a long time now
she has put things off,

made space for herself
to think.
On the bed
she muses on her feelings
as if she were bathing
and feelings were water
she cupped and poured over her.
She feels clean, free, soft.
When she looks out the window
at a great space of blue sky
she thinks of the coming child,
the voice, the laughter
that will resonate through her life.
How strange the world is,
the bloodshed and war and hate,
when there is such a thing as birth.
The child comes as softly as snowfall
and across the perfectly even field of his fate
makes his tracks and direction known.
She is the house on which the snow falls.
How strange and wonderful and terrible it all is.
In her belly the baby forms like a cloud,
its hands become five leaf clovers. The skin connects
and grafts. It becomes its own world, a small earth,
circling in the gravity of two adults.
He will come like a thunderstorm
filling the mountain gorges with his songs.
And yet, he will not harm the flower.
When he is old enough to leave his mother,
it will be the first winter she truly feels the cold.

* * * *

We bought a small house
along the river, in Southside barrio.
A shack I pried boards from the door to get in—

half-acre of land in the back
heaped with decades of scrap—rusted wire fencing, creosote
railroad ties, tumbleweeds, a mountain of decaying
harvest never picked, weaving itself
slowly into the dirt again.

                             I gutted the plaster frame house,
nailed, puttied, roofed, plumbed,
poured cement, sheet-rocked, tiled, carpeted,
tore-out, re-set,
                  piled, burned, cleaned, cemented, installed,
washed and painted,
trimmed, pruned, shoveled, raked,
                  sawed, hammered, measured, stuccoed,
until,
              calloused handed, muscle-firmed, sleek hard bodied,
                    our small house rose
                    from a charred, faded gravemarker,
                    a weather-rotted roost
                    for junkies and vagrants,

wind, rain, and sun splintered
jagged stories of storms on,
I corrected,
                  re-wrote upon
                  this plaster-wood tablet,
                  our own version of love, family and power.

                    *   *   *   *

Afternoon of March 21st, I helped
Gabriela into our Falcon,
and we drove the pre-planned route
to the mid-wife's house.

Contractions—
              push and breathe,
                        harder and harder—
I daubed her forehead
with a cool washcloth,
squatted with her,
told her jokes about Texans.

              Arched back—
                        strained spine, swelled pelvis–
                                  fingers clenching sheet–
Fertility dance of woman.
              Surge up and plunge down–
                        grit teeth–
                                  then, a muzzled, deep drum beat
groan,
and from bloodnet and bonebed
birthslimed, fleshgusted, slipsurged

              brown baby   aaagggg-aaagggging
into my hands,
as I kissed his wet head and welcomed my son Pablo into the world.

I stepped outside on the porch,
a storm had just subsided—
              black leaves stuck to red bricks,
              moon shimmering medallions
              in wet-street pools.
Ah, mijito,
              you were a long green tree limb
              in another world.
When Gabriela and I made love,
              wind, heaving wind, plundered you.
You came to us,
              and now roam,
              with blood-gorged feelings,

in the clearing of your mother's stomach,
                              rest your body,
as you nibble at the dark grass
of her breast.

I went inside
took Pablito from Gabriela
to let her sleep and rest,
then circled my arm around your body Pablo,
as we slept in the bed next to mama,
I promised you and all living things,

                    I would never abandon you.

                *   *   *   *

Meditations on the South Valley

I

Disbelief
numbed me
as we turned the corner.
Hard, dark calm
swelled in my body
braced for a shock.
At the far end of the curving road
the fire engine's
wheel-light unspun red/red/red/
into the night.

White hands
of gray smoke greeted us
from the charred husk
of our house.
Neighbors and firemen
blurred past.
My son sleeping in the back seat—
my wife rushed out
while I sat with him.

Blind to the dull glimmers
of axes and shovels,
thick hoses unwheeled
on silver reels—
deaf to the urgent, shouting voices
and crackling walkie-talkies,
to the rubber-coated men
boots sloshing back and forth
in black wet muck—

                                        I thought,

my poems!
10 years of poems

cocooned in pages
unfolded their flaming wings
in silky smoke
and fluttered past blackened rafters.

My wife's face dazed
by the destruction.
"Oh, Martín, it's all gone."
She carried our son
across the road to a neighbor's house.

After everyone left
I sloshed through the rooms.
Scorched rubble and black flakes.
It was a haunted house
brooding in its own black rebellion.

On hands and knees
I sifted through
the lush nest of ashes
in my writing room.

For hours I stood there
in silence, listening to the darkness.
Black breath of roof boards
weakly smoldering
the end
of all the cities and peoples
I had become.

*   *   *   *

II

Forced by circumstances
to live in this Heights apartment—
how strangely clean and new
these white walls are,
thin orange carpet
that sprawls through every room
like a rat's
red faded wrinkled brain
pulsating noises
from tenants below.
The ceramic faces of women
who live here,
and buddha-cheeked men
who all wear straw hats
to walk their poodles,
manicured and clipped elegant
as heirloom dinnerware
glittering beneath chandeliers—

I don't want
to live here
among the successful. To the South Valley
the white dove of my mind flies,
searching for news of life.

*   *   *   *

III

En verdad, no conozco la gente.
Oh, I see them—Mr. García
walking here along the acequia,
his face worn and silent,
smiles at me with a strong set of white teeth.
Freddy, el cholo, revs
his '62 Impala beneath the shade of an elm tree
in his yard.
I don't know the names
of those who take walks across weedy fields at dusk
and wave to me.
La gente del Southside
give nothing away
except what one sees. The inside
of their lives
is filled with white lights
and rich brewing coffees.
They have opened their lives to me
over the years,
and I have wavered for strength
to accept,
and then have gone down, down
into the green jungly growths
of their worlds
to become one of them.

*　*　*　*

IV

Send me news Rafa
of the pack dogs sleeping
in wrecked cars in empty yards,
or los veteranos
dreaming in their whiskey bottles
on porches
of the past, full of glory and fear.
The black smell of wet earth
seeps into old leaning adobes,
and prowls like a black panther through open windows.
Austere-faced hombres
hoeing their jardines
de chile y maíz in the morning,
crush beer cans and stuff them in gunny sacks
and pedal on rusty bicycles
in the afternoon to the recycling scale,
and at Coco's chante
at dusk tecatos se juntan,
la cocina jammed like the stock exchange lobby,
as los vatos raise their fingers
indicating cuánto quieren.
There is much more I miss Rafa,
so send me news.

*   *   *   *

V

Sunset over the black water of the Río Grande.
It means something to me.
My soul flutters like a black wing
every time I cross the Río Grande bridge.
Crows in cottonwoods
form a long black waving path,
rustling along the horizon.
An old drunk squirms under the bridge
to drink his quart of COORS.
Pack dogs roam—Chicanos cruise in Monte Carlos—
the dead eavesdrop at windows
on women talking at kitchen tables—
children holler in dusty games on dirt roads—
the moon blazes warmly on black water
of the Río Grande.

VI

Cruising back from 7-11
esta mañana
in my '56 Chevy troquita,
beat up ranckled
farm truck,
clanking between rows
of new shiny cars—

"Hey fella! Trees need pruning
and the grass needs trimming!"
A man yelled down to me
from his 3rd-story balcony.

"Sorry, I'm not the gardener,"
I yelled up to him.

Funny how in the Valley
an old truck symbolizes prestige
and in the Heights, poverty.

Worth is determined in the Valley
by age and durability,
and in the Heights, by newness
and impression.

In the Valley,
the atmosphere is soft and worn,
things are shared and passed down.
In the Heights,
the air is blistered with the glaze
of new cars and new homes.

How many days of my life
I have spent fixing up

rusty broken things,
charging up old batteries,
wiring pieces of odds and ends together!
Ah, those lovely bricks
and sticks I found in fields
and took home with me
to make flower boxes!
The old cars I've worked on
endlessly giving them tune-ups,
changing tires, tracing
electrical shorts,
cursing when I've been stranded
between Laguna pueblo and Burque.
It's the process of making-do,
of the life I've lived between
breakdowns and break-ups, that has made life
worth living.

I could not bear a life
with everything perfect.

* * * *

VII

When the sun
slants through my bedroom window
in this apartment,
I think how there is nothing to do.
Where's the kindling
for the stove?
Or the stucco and stain to patch
the portal?

My legs feel like a black-toothed
abuelita
hunched in manta at the bus stop.
I wait
for something to do . . .

> in the Valley at my house
> y parcelita de tierra,
> I added, raised, knocked down,
> until over months and years,
> the place in which I lived
> had my own character.
> I could look at it and see
> myself.

This apartment
reflects a faceless person,
   with no future,
      no past,
         just an emptiness.

*　*　*　*

VIII

Late night movie.
I can't sleep.
A bandit
in an old western movie
jumps from a saloon roof
onto his horse
and gallops into the llano.
My heart is an old post
dreams I tied to it years ago
yank against
to get free.
I turn the tv off
and in the darkness,   let them go—

                    a chavalo riding his bicycle
                    at dawn down Barcelona road,
                    clenching roses in his teeth,
in the handle-bar basket
are apples he took from random trees on the road.

*   *   *   *

IX

Eddie blew his head off
playing chicken
with his brother. Para proof
he was man,
he blew his head off.
Don't toll the bell brother,
'cuz he was not religious.
The gray donkey he liked to talk to
at Dead-Man's Corner
grazes sadly. Eddie's gone, its black-lashed dark eyes
mourn. His tío Manuel shatters a bottle
of La Copita wine against the adobe wall
where he and his compas drink every afternoon,
and Manuel weeps for Eddie.

> "He was the kid without a coat
> during winter. 'Member he stole
> those gloves from SEARS, you 'member,
> he stole those gloves? Nice gloves.
> He gave 'em to me ese."

Blew his head off.
The explosion of the gun
was the golden flash of his voice
telling us *no more, no more, no more.*
His last bloody words
water the dried weeds
where his jefa threw the stucco fragments
out. Sparrows peck his brains outside
by the fence posts.

> Flaco said, "Don't give him no eulogy!
> He was for brothers and sisters
> in struggle. You know I saw him
> in court one day, when they handcuffed

his older brother to take his brother
to prison, you know Eddie jumped the
benches, and grabbed his brother's
handcuffs, yelling, don't take my brother
he is not a bad man!"

Everybody in Southside knew Eddie,
little Eddie, bad little Eddie.
He treated everybody with respect and honor.
With black-board classroom attention
he saw injustice, hanging out en las calles,
sunrise 'til sunset, with the bros and sisters.

Don't ring the bell, brother.
Let it lie dead.
Let the heavy metal rust.
Let the rope fray and swing mutely
in the afternoon dust and wind.

How many times they beat you Eddie?
How many police clubs
are smeared with your blood,
Switch blade en bolsa,
manos de piedra,
en la línea con sus carnales,
to absorb the tire-jack beatings from other locotes,
    billy-club beatings de la jura—
your blood Eddie spotted
sidewalks,
smeared shovel handles,
coated knife blades,
blurred your eyes and painted your body
in a tribal-barrio dance
to set yourself free,
to know what was beyond the boundaries
you were born into,

in your own way,
in your own sweet way, taking care
of grandma, her room giving off the aura
of a saintly relic,
old wood floors and walls
smoothed by the continual passing of her body,
burnished to an altar of sorts,
in which she was your saint,
you cared for,
eating with her each evening,
sharing the foodstamps she had,
walking her to la tiendita,
whose walls were scribbled with black paint
your handwriting and initials,
your boundary marker, deadly symbol to other chavos
entering your barrio—the severe, dark stitches of letters
on the walls
healed your wound at being illiterate—
the white adobe wall with your cholo symbols
introduced you to the world,
                as Eddie
who leaned on haunches in the sun,
back against a wall,
talking to 11, 13, 15, 17 year old vatos
sniffing airplane glue
from a paper bag,
breathing in typing correction fluid,
smoking basucón, what Whites call crack,
smoking pelo rojo sinsemilla:
                        you listened to their words,
                        chale
                        simón
                        wacha bro
                        me importa madre
                        ni miedo de la muerta
                        ni de la pinta
                        ni de la placa,

and you cried out
hijo de la chingada madre,
cansao
de retablos de calles
pintaos con sangre de tu gente,
                                        you cried out
to stop it!
Quit giving the wind our grief stricken voices
at cemeteries,
quit letting the sun soak up our blood,
quit dropping out of high school,
                            in the center of the storm,
you absorbing the feeling of worthlessness,
caught in your brown skin
and tongue that could not properly pronounce English words,
caught like a seed unable to plant itself,
                            you picked up God's blue metal face
and scattered the seed of your heart
across the afternoon air,
among the spiked petals of a cactus,
and elm leaves,
                        your voice whispered
                        in the dust and weeds,
a terrible silence,
not to forget your death.

X

Barrio Southside
used to be called
Los Ranchos de Atrisco
eighty years ago. Before that,
Río Abajo. Names change.

Dawn arrives,
shimmering like a hammered tin santito,
dangling from a viga portal, tic-tic,
clicking in the breeze against stucco & adobe.

I study the faces of boys
playing in dirt yards,
and see Cuauhtémoc—images
that reflect gold-cuts
engraved on medallions
in Spanish museums.

Vatos,
eyes sleek with dreams,
lounge on porches
reading the flight of geese
above the Río Grande,
look like Netzahualcóyotl.

And thrashing out from the bosque's
wall of trees and wild bushes,
see a man in threadbare clothing,
work-worn muscles,
eyes weathered as war-drum skins,
his skin glowing with sweat
like rain on old rocks,

and here, you see
a distant relative
of Aztec warriors.

*   *   *   *

XI

Things change.
Pseudo Spanish-style apartments
now loom on the east mesa.
Used to be land grant tierra.
Now retired Texan ranchers park
their Revcon travel-homes,
pampering them like prize bulls.
The other morning
Mr. Churner's grandson came to visit him.
Mr. Churner shouldered a saw-horse
out to the parking-lot
next to his chromed bull,
and tottering on new boots, he threw
the rope six times, missing the imagined cow,
and his grandson walked to retrieve
the rope six times,
watching his grandfather's face redden
with each toss.
Slumped shouldered, wobbly footed,
angular old withering cowboy,
Mr. Churner turns, shouldering the saw-horse
back onto the apartment patio.
Sipping his tea in his lawn chair,
in his face I see a man who scowls,

> "I made a goddamn mistake,
> selling out. Hell, I'd give anything,
> for a nice, cold, tall
> glass of well water."

*   *   *   *

XII

I am remembering the South Valley.
Rain smacked tin-roofs
like an all night passenger train,
fiery flames of moon flashing
from the smoke stack.
Beneath the rain shaded sky,
faint surge of rain pulsing down my windows,
rain's blue mouth curling around everything,
                              I dream
myself maíz root
swollen in pregnant earth,
rain seeping into my black bones
sifting red soil grains of my heart
into earth's hungry mouth.

I am part of the earth.

*   *   *   *

XIII

Antonio, you want to say something
with your polished brown-wood eyes.
Your legs bend to steady you
on the unseen horse. You turn your head back
to see me, then go
into red hills of sunlight
in the backyard, down curving paths
of moss and fire,
awake the sleeping Goddess of Dirt,
to plant your yellow flower soul
in her mouth
with a stick.

My son,
                    your eyes
are music storms,
filled with the black song of earth,
your heart's reddened eye
peers at a blue alfalfa flower,
glowing with your destiny.

*   *   *   *

XIV

El Pablo was a bad dude.
Presidente of the River Rats
(700 strong), from '67 to '73.
Hands so fast
he could catch two flies buzzing
in air, and still light his cigarette.
From a flat foot standing position
he jumped to kick the top of a door jamb
twice with each foot.
Pants and shirt creased and cuffed,
sharp pointy shoes polished to black glass,
El Pachucón was cool to the bone, brutha.
His initials were etched
on Junior High School desks,
Castañeda's Meat Market walls,
downtown railway bridge,
on the red bricks at the Civic Auditorium,
Uptown & Downtown,
El Pachucón left his mark.
Back to the wall, legs crossed, hands pocketed,
combing his greased-back ducktail
when a jaine walked by. Cool to the huesos.
Now he's a janitor at Pajarito
Elementary School—

> still hangs out
> by the cafeteria, cool to the bone,
> el vato,
> still wears his sunglasses,
> still proud,

he leads a new gang of neighborhood parents
to the Los Padilla Community Center
to fight against polluted ground water,
against Developers who want to urbanize
his rural running grounds.

Standing in the back of the crowd
last Friday, I saw Pablo stand up
and yell at the Civic Leaders from City Hall,

        "Listen cuates, you pick your weapons.
        We'll fight you on any ground you pick."

XV

As a niño I believed
God carved my grandfather in a few minutes.
He was rough-cut—
thick-knubby field working hands,
his face a ball of maíz dough
wind and sun fingers had kneaded
into a calm, bronzed, kind face.
On his spindle-backed chair
outside the door on the dirt,
he mumbled psalms in Spanish.
Sitting next to his massive, black, scuffed workboots,
I could wade into his brown water words,
float at his feet looking up to the sky—

       in the distance
       I could hear someone chopping wood,
       and smell the heat wavering off stones,
       and sense the loneliness that brimmed
       from adobe houses at dusk—

a loneliness
no one could see, that I sensed
in a horse's tail,
a cow's glum, dumb look, or in the lizard's
blinding scurry into weeds.
A loneliness that glided over my grandfather's
oily, sweat-stained fieldworker's hat,
with red wings, I hooped away
with waving arms, like a vaquero hoops
a few stray vacas back into the herd,

       I twirled and skipped and hooped
         every morning, for the old, dark-skinned man,
who gave me a smile as he walked to work.

XVI

Jefe,
todavía no saben . . .

Under color of race
on your death certificate,
they have you down
as White.

You fought against that
label
all your short life, jefe,
and now they have you down
as White.

They had you down
when you lived, down
because you were too brown.

Dead on arrival
when you tried to be White.
You were brown as empty whiskey bottles,
and your accent was brown adobe dirt
you shattered bottles against.

Dead now,
you are White.
Under specify suicide or homicide,
I scribbled out accident and wrote in
Suicide—
scribbled out White and wrote in
Chicano. Erased caused by aspiration of meat
and wrote in
trying to be White.

* * * *

XVII

I love the wind
when it blows through my barrio.
It hisses its snake love
down calles de polvo,
and cracks egg-shell skins
of abandoned homes.
Stray dogs find shelter
along the river,
where great cottonwoods rattle
like old covered wagons,
stuck in stagnant waterholes.
Days when the wind blows
full of sand and grit,
men and women make decisions
that change their whole lives.
Windy days in the barrio
give birth to divorce papers
and squalling separation. The wind tells us
what others refuse to tell us,
informing men and women of a secret,
that they move away to hide from.

*　*　*　*

XVIII

La curandera Feliz
wears her blue rebozo,
its threads tracing frayed conclusions
on life,
down her arms and leafless head.
Face etched by Spirits
she conjures
on the ditchbank,
she listens to wild sermons
of black birds in the elms.

My tía Gabriela told me
la curandera Feliz brews
herbs, spatters mud on her face,
burns powdery leaves
at the foot of a long mirror,
and as the room fills with herbal aroma
and leaf-loam smolders secrets,
Feliz gazes into her bubbling
scrubbed silver pots and pans,
and foretells the future.

She draws children close to her
and her words are as soft as a dawn sprinkle-shower
over their green wild-grass hearts.
With adults, faint white light
fills her eyes, and slowly, her words rise
through a thousand years of sleep.

Me 'cuerdo Caspar The Ghost—
aquel vato de Duranes
que andaba tirando broncas
pa' cual lao.
Fíjate, que aquella vieja brujona

le dio un cambio.
After a visita to her chante,
se apagó el foco.

As if he rises from the tomb every morning,
Caspar stands on the Rio Grande bridge,
foto de Cristo in one hand, New Testament
in the other, held high, facing them
toward the traffic flow,
mumbling curses to us pobres.

Outside his cantón, an old condemned barnwood
shack leaning haphazardly in an alley,
Caspar tacks hundreds of pictures
of Christ with the bleeding-thorned heart,
to ward off worldly evils.

Who knows what la curandera Feliz
did to him.

* * * *

XIX

Don't go out with María
Clemente, she is a bruja.
I am telling you—
Pablo told me of the things
she did to him, to make him stay with her—

She wrapped a single long strand
of her black hair
around the inside of his penis ridge;
she melted wax & ashes
over his letters and photographs,
placed them in a black box,
& chanted over them under a full moon.
She spat a piece of toenail
into his mouth when they were making love,
hoping he would swallow it;
often times at night, naked under the sheets,
he would awake clear-minded from a dead sleep,
find her chanting over him,
a corner of the sheet tucked between her thighs,
she rubbed and prayed to the moon.

Laugh Clemente,
but I warn you, you will be like Pablo soon.
He drank to ease his forced imprisonment.
One night, driving South-14,
Pablo and María were returning from a dance.
She screamed for him to slow down.
He went faster down the curving road.
They went airborne
at a 15mph curve
Pablo hit going 55. He was drunk. She crouched
on the floorboard, screaming for him to stop.
He remembers saying to her
before they crashed,

"So you do not want to let me go?
Is this what you want,
that we both die? Then we will!"
The car came to a sudden
crashing halt in a field.
They survived. Next day Pablo went walking
down the road and never returned to her.

Take my word Clemente, María has powerful magic, carnal.
Mucho cuidao. Do not wear the pouch around your neck
she will offer you—do not.

*　*　*　*

XX

Tengo mucho respeto pa'
los viejos de mi barrio.
They hobble out a creaking door
to hoe and rake their garden plot.
They've survived kill-dem-meskin days,
retained their humor for a good joke,
and slowly wean themselves
from this life,
and prepare for the next—
                    they pull their rosaries out
                    and put away their pictures
                    of women in bathing suits,
they sign their names to church
donor journals,
tear up old phone numbers
of old girlfriends in their wallets,
                    strip off the paper
                    from their Army suits in closets,
                    and no longer stop at Manuel's cantina
                    for a drink.
On a stump in their yard,
during the afternoon siesta, they wait
for La Muerte to arrive,
in black cape, red feathered headdress,
red lava face glowing,
jeweled in turquoise and obsidian
from neck to wrists,
black diamond glittering navel,
feet of eagle claws, legs staunch
and furred as a jaguar's,
her voice a blue dark winter dawn,
that slowly numbs them,
until they leave wrinkled bodies of flowers
withering on the stump.

These are the viejos
who endured poverty,
and learned to do
with what they had,
and made a rich dream land
out of a small garden plot.

*   *   *   *

XXI

Ayer, there was a bronca
at Tingly Beach.
Vatos de Sanjo, leaning on their ranflas
con puertas painted with baby-dolls,
contra Southside locos,
Virgen de Guadalupe tattooed on their pechos.
Nobody won.
After switchblades and tire-irons cooled,
steel prides softened,
great brooding clouds darkened the sky
and everybody went home.
After Tingly was deserted, I went back
and threw popcorn to the ducks.
Branch tips of cottonwoods trembled
as they surveyed the battleground.
Sparrows quipped off quick warnings
of reasons why brothers fight brothers.
The heavy tongue of rain lolled down
licking the bloody earth
like a lioness her wounded cub.
Rugged jaws of the Sandía mountains
to east crackled lightning.

I sat in my low-rider
while illimitable beads of rain
beat my windshield, popped off the hood,
and swirled over dirt and pavement,
mixing in with blood.

What point was proved by 7 Chicanos
stabbed?

                              I thought,
                   vatos de la noche y de las calles,
                   camaradas hasta la muerte,

sin plata en la bolsa,
sin miedo de la pinta,
hijos de la chingada madre,
dando esquina en cualquier movida o pedo,
firmes, corazones firmes.

They lead lives trying to decide
who they are going to be—
Do they stand on Plymouth Rock
and defiantly stare down on La Raza?
Or under the fierce glare oᶠ sun
in the Aztlán desert, do they endure
their thirst for acceptance and success?
Do they celebrate Columbus day
or invent their own Día de Cortez?

Ann Bradstreet never wrote of their suffering
eloquently as Gabriela Mistral,
and Southern tobacco plantations
never smelled as good as Analco corn fields,
nor did the Hudson sparkle as gaily
in the morning as does the Río Grande.

But growing up they will find
these things out.
Perhaps in a prison cell, or stooping
over a pots-n-pans sink
in a restaurant,
or in a field picking corn,
the dark fuzziness of what they've been told
in history books
will fade, and beyond the borders
of their fears, they will see their own faces
in the mesquite tree,
    in the Río Grande agua,
        in the black mesas,
            in the twisting arroyos—

These Cholos y Vatos Locos
who have refused to let themselves
be put down,
and lifted in this poem-photograph
smiling, knowing who they are,
                    they let the slow blue water
                    of their souls
                    seep back into the brown soil of their lives,
to speak their own lives in green,
under the harsh and punishing light of Burque.

*   *   *   *

XXII

In June I went searching
for isolated apricot trees.
In a blue baseball cap, ragged sneakers,
faded jeans and t-shirt,
while old men and women
threw hot loops of tortillas on the comal,
I crossed alfalfa fields,
ruffling black birds out of cottonwoods
with dirt clods I threw.
Garbage trucks growled and stuffed their steel stomachs
at dumpsters, restaurant trashcans,
and green, lawn-trimmed residential blocks,
while I skipped through alleys
pocketing old pennies and rubber balls.
The sun slowly moved
with the weight of its years
across the sky. Old trees threw black capes
of shade, under which I rested.
I climbed over tottering old post fences,
brushed my cheeks with dew-wet rose leaves,
and for minutes stood mesmerized
by the dark gleams of black feathers
floating in brown murky ditch water.

Innocently, I drifted and slipped
through the day
like a sparrow flying off from a telephone line
into the open sky, falling
from the sky upon a butter wrapper
or piece of tortilla on the ground.

I'd sit on bent fenders
in open fields and eat my apricots.
At dusk I would make my way back

to my barrio, unroll my blanket
under Isleta bridge, and crouch
into plump sleep,
like a piece of drift wood
settling in weeds, my dreams were filled
with talking frogs, giant crickets,
godly flies, with the yellow, brooding eyelid of the moon
flickering at me sensuously.

*   *   *   *

XXIII

Pancho, the barrio idiot.
Rumor is that una bruja from Bernalillo
le embrujo. Unshaven, chattering
and nodding to airy friends
that follow him,
he roams the barrio all day.
I see him at least twice a day—
walking on the ditch behind my house,
hours later walking across the bridge.

Harmless, la gente leave him alone
in his own fantasies,
to share his bread with invisible companions,
to speak back to voices
that brim over from his childhood memories.

I have seen him
on all fours in Raúl's field
with the sheep. Or last Christmas
in the tree meowing like a cat.
You always fill my heart Pancho
with delight.

* * * *

XXIV

Mejicanos at A Mi Gusto cantina
on Coors Rd.,
spend their pay on 20-20 Mad Dog wine,
sit in the back of pick-ups
in the parking lot, damn their destinies
and curse Chicanos.
Wine is like mother's voice
that soothes their sadness
and explains misfortunes.

Dawn they all go with shovels,
rakes and hoes,
to work Mr. Chamber's chile, alfalfa and corn fields.
Their shovels are crosses they carry.

Each night their heads fall
drunkenly to the side
as flies clot wine dribbling
from their mouth corners.

Men who have lived on rations
for so long, who came hidden in car trunks,
thin, sweaty, frightened,
working for dollars to buy knives and beer,
and small plastic packets sold in grocery stores—
a tin plate, cup, spoon, and fork, painted Army green,
they can carry in a paper sack when the crop is picked.

They dream in drunken stupors,
of Mejicles,
of a return to Juárez where they sold
fruta from wooden carts.
But no—

                    at dawn,

they awake on a floor,
still dreaming of a new truck,
of sending money home to Torreón or Durango,
to sisters and brothers
they have not seen in six years.

Taut, thin dark arms
strain at the hoe,
their backs cluster together like centipede legs,
bending and winding down rows of chile,
their dark fuzzy faces under straw hats
bobbing in the afternoon heat waves.

Their dreams fade
like red hot wires, overheated
burnt generator coils,
and passing one in the store,
look into their eyes and see black anger,
smell the heavy smoke of their skin
and muscles ready to burst into flames.

* * * *

XXV

Benny drowned today in the Río Grande.
After drinking a few beers
with Louey y Fernando,
cabuleando on la playa como vatos do,
he swam out poco pedo.
El Agua was in a mood of lust.
Mean shadowy crevices of moss
yearned,
tree-roots and shag-grass
blackened hair on the Water's face,
as it became a gold mask
with two obsidian eyes,
                    opening its mouth to swallow Benny,
crushing his young brown body
in its swaying-blue claws,
clawing it to the bottom with sledge-hammer hits.

El Agua drank him in deliriously,
adopted Benny as part of its familia,
gasping at the murky bottom,
until the last small bubbles throbbed to the top,
hung limp on surface and swayed away on gray currents.

They found him downstream
days later by Belén, swollen, at a bank
slushing in swamp twigs, grass, and weeds.
Packs of wild perros
feated on him, and gnawed the puffy white tortilla
of his belly, arms and neck.
He dreamed in the mud and water.
Staggering away with grief
and anger, his jefito Benito Chávez screamed
at El Agua of the Río Grande,

raised his arms pleading with the water
to give back his only son.

Pero el Benny murió hoy
todo el barrio was saying
the day they found him dead.
On porches guitarristas sang death songs,
and old viejas prayed for his soul
before their small altars in bedrooms,
At paint & body shops
vatos locos milling outside were saying,

>   ". . . el vato thought
>   he could swim across,
>   y luego un current
>   le pescó y le tumbó."

At Casa Armijo Community Center,
el Ernie said,

>   ". . . el Agua was switching
>   Benny back and forth like a rag
>   shook out after dusting."

At gas stations & auto parts stores
that litter Isleta, la gente were saying,

>   "Estaba gacho, More he hit and kicked el Agua,
>   más que la Muerte le 'garró. Bien gacho bro,
>   te digo."

>   ". . . lo que flipió el swiche, fue cuando
>   we were standing on the playa, ése. Benny
>   yelled ayúdame! ayúdame! The air turned cold,
>   cold ése, bien frío."

At St. Ann's church, los vatos that knew
el Benny, and came for his rosario,
said,

". . . bien firme el Benny, muy 'uena gente
el vato. His cora y alma will be with warriors
under the earth. He was chosen to be sacrificed
ese, como los Aztecas al sol, pues,
al Agua. Asina es, asina es, our lives I mean."

Day after his funeral,
viejas hung laundry together
and sighed about his death,
viejos hoed their weeds
and felt sorry for Benny's jefe.
Graffiti on grocery-store walls
and laundry mats
warned others away from el Agua,
". . . es donde vive La Muerte . . ."

And on and on
the Río Grande flows,
a fast spinning roulette wheel,
spinning past lives
until, it points a brown fingering wave
to another body, and drops it
like a black marble
into its silver swirling mouth.

*   *   *   *

XXVI

We cut down the elm tree today.
Ungiving, old ancient tusk of trunk.
John straddled branches,
stepping through seed-bud sticks,
breaking dead limbs. His head was lost
in branches—
                        chainsaw dangling from his waist rope,
                        he slowly towed up,
                        pulled the cord,
                        crackling, it snarled saw dust down
                                        through
                                                the air.

Limbs crashed down
with shuddering groans and cracking throes,
hit the ground with dead thuds,
trembling air they fell through.

Wrinkled chunks of hide bark
growled down. John worked his way down
from the upper most branches,
down to its thick mane—
                        wedge-cutting ten feet at a time,
                        flat cutting from the opposite end;
slowly the main trunk tipped, lean-creaked, sucking air
thrashing down, bellowing
with one massive blow and fall,
breathing one last leaf-heave, like an elephant
grounded, the trembling crash became silent.

Where the tree had stood
a silver waterfall of sky now poured down.
Still air.

Red dusk. I felt I had just killed
an old man.

*   *   *   *

XXVII

We started on the house.
At first there was the black mass
of garbage—
                    loading burned rubbish
                    en la troquita.
Countless loads stacked high above the sides,
bulging sooty wreckage
waddling at each bend on La Vega Rd.,
overload springs gruntling
at dirt-ribs and pot-holes
pa'l dompe.

                    Two weeks hauling garbage.
                    Ten years of my ashes.
Then we stood, afraid and confused,
before the skeletal house
wondering how we were going to build it.
Meiyo looked into my eyes
and I knew he was thinking of the war
that enflamed my writing room,
of the villages of peoples gone,
                    and he yelled, with love-voice of a brother,
                            "Let's get started."
With nail bars, hammers, axes,
we stripped and thinned the house down,
like a tailor measuring a bride-to-be,
and tore sinks out,
closets out,
windows out,
until Dale, Meiyo & I sipped coffee one afternoon,
and Meiyo said,
                    "Now call for the new lumber—
                    and throw those damn plans away Martín,
                            we don't need 'em."

Reusing old lumber (what we could),
according to Meiyo's vision code,
(how he hated tract-housing, how he wanted my house
to be gentle and soft, with the comforts of trees and sunshine seen,
light space and airiness in each room),
he directed the rafters, cripples, studs,
headers—

        balancing twenty feet high
        on a single 2 × 2 joist,
        we handed Meiyo the cathedral ceiling rafters,
        they spread
towering great lengths across from wall to outside wall,
then we built the non-bearing walls,
windows, skylight tunnels,
breezes and sky fell upon—

        adding another bathroom,
        another master bedroom with fireplace,
        and slowly the house took on
        unbelievable strength and elegance.

Bones bummed on blistering 16 hour a day work,
we squinted our sawdusted eyes,
pushed our sore-aching muscles,
dry-gutted bellies, sour mouthed,
working non-stop,
haggard, calloused men,
we cursed at sheetrock,
coughed at paint spray and clogged spray guns,
damned out & in nails and board corners
to catch and fit,
growled a hundred times, sweaty & mean-tempering
our way forth.

        After that, the interior of the house
emanating blue dawn light,
full of gusto in the fresh-timber smelling house,
proud of the 3 bedrooms, hallway, livingroom & kitchen,

my finest poem I thought,
that sheltered me from the rain and wind,
as we worked our way
into doors, staining kickboards, putting doorknobs in,
(fine-tuning the poem),
measuring cabinets, leveling the floors,
shimmying here & there,
spitting & stomping, throwing our tools down in disgust
and huffs of temper,
yelling into the cold mornings
at each other, trying to go on and finish
in six weeks.

Eddie came and helped stucco, (in between complaints),
Ralphie ran heating ducts, (in between taking care of his pimp business),
Rocky taped and floated, (in between scoring his chiva),
Caspar ran the wire, (in between dreaming Dialing For Dollars would call him),
and Manuel plumbed.

           After the texture,
                 our rhythms eased, slid from fierce
determination to a sleepy cat's mellowness,
relief, and light-heartedness.
           More coffee breaks, later arrivals,
breakfast at Merlinda's restaurant on me,
a few more loads of grubbing scrap lumber to the dump,
and we stood back and breathed deep—

                    it was done.

*   *   *   *

XXVIII

In this Heights apartment
I became lonely for the South Valley.
Images drifted by in my brain
          this tree—
            esa piedra—
              aquel fiel y caballo—
                santuario de los penitentes on La Vega rd.—
the darkness swaddling
las calles con polvo
niños kicked up at play.

People live out real lives in the South Valley.
Tin can lids patch adobe walls,
the moon through a window
smolders at St. Francis' statue feet
on a dresser,
and there is a quietness heavy as blood
that spills over into each afternoon,
and brims like flame over the fields.

            My house burned
            and we re-built it.
I felt hurt, yes . . .
and grieved with the shovel of ashes,
the ashes heaped on the truck,
and drove it to the dump with a numb sense of duty
I had to do,
full of loss and grief, and joy
that I was able to create
                another house,
                a child in its own image.
I gave birth to a house.
It came, cried from my hands, sweated from my body,
ached from my gut and back. I was stripped down to the essential

Glossary I:

Line Translations from the Text

p. 11 Tú sabes, nos pusimos bien chatos. *You know, we were very drunk.*

p. 12 Dios mío cómo llorabas. / A veces your jefito . . . *My God, how you cried. / At times your father . . .*

p. 12 "¿Dónde está tu mamá? . . . / Se casó otra vez y tiene dos niños. No, / no te puedo decir dónde viven." *"Where is your mother? . . . / She's married again and has two children. No, / I cannot tell you where they live."*

p. 56 En verdad, no conozco la gente. *To tell the truth, I don't know the people.*

p. 64 . . . en bolsa, / manos de piedra, / en la línea con sus carnales. . . . *in his pocket, / hands of stone, / standing the line with his brothers.*

p. 65 chale / simón / wacha bro / me importa madre / ni miedo de la muerta / ni de la pinta / ni de la placa. *no / yes / look at this man / I don't give a damn / nor am I afraid of death / nor of prison / nor of the badge.*

p. 66 hijo de la chingada madre, / cansao / de retablos de calles / pintaos con sangre de tu gente. *son of the cursed mother, / I'm tired / of street altars / painted with the blood of your people.*

p. 75 Jefe, / todavía no saben . . . *Father, / they still don't know . . .*

pp. 77-78 Me 'cuerdo Caspar the Ghost— / aquel vato de Duranes / que andaba tirando broncas / pa' cual lao. / Fíjate, que aquella vieja brujona / le dio un cambio. / After a visita to her chante, / se apagó el foco. *I remember Caspar the Ghost— / that guy from Duranes / who went around fighting / every which way. / Check it out, that old witch / changed him. / After a visit to her house, / the light in his head went out.*

p. 81   Tengo mucho respeto pa' / los viejos de mi barrio. *I have much respect for / the old people in my neighborhood.*

pp. 83-84   Vatos de la noche y de las calles, / camaradas hasta la muerte, / sin plata en la bolsa / sin miedo de la pinta / hijos de la chingada madre, / dando esquina en cualquier movida o pedo, / firmes, corazones firmes. *Men of the night and of the streets, / comrades until death, / with no money in their pockets, / without fear of prison, / sons of the cursed mother, / giving back-up in whatever schemes or trouble, / strong, strong hearts.*

p. 91   cabuleando on la playa como vatos do, / he swam out poco pedo. *horsing around on the beach the way guys do, / he swam out a little drunk.*

p. 92   y luego un current / le pescó y le tumbó. *and then a current / picked him up and turned him over.*

p. 92   "Estaba gacho, More he hit and kicked el Agua, / más que la Muerte le garró. Bien gacho bro, / te digo." / ". . . lo que flipió el swiche, fue cuando / we were standing on the playa, ése. Benny / yelled ayúdame! ayúdame! / The air turned cold, / cold ése, bien frío." *"It was bad, the more he hit and kicked the water, / the more Death clutched him. Cold blooded bro, / I tell you." / ". . . what changed it was when / we were standing on the beach, man. Benny / yelled help me! help me! / The air turned cold, / it was cold, very cold."*

pp. 92-93   ". . . bien firme el Benny, muy 'uena gente / el vato. His cora y alma will be with warriors / under the earth. He was chosen to be sacrificed / ése, como los Aztecas al sol, pues, / al Agua. Asina es, asina es, our lives I mean." *". . . Benny was strong, he was good / people. His heart and soul will be with warriors / under the earth. He was chosen to be sacrificed / man, like the Aztecs to the sun, well, / to the water. That's the way it is, that's the way it is, our lives I mean."*

p. 99   esa piedra— / aquel fiel y caballo— / santuario de los penitentes on La Vega rd.—*that stone— / that field and horse— / the penitents' sanctuary on La Vega Road—*

[102]

Glossary II:

abuelita: grandmother
acequía: irrigation ditch

Barelas: Chicano neighborhood in Albuquerque
borrachera: the drinking life
bronca: a fight or scuffle
bruja: witch
canale: rain spout
chale: no way (*slang*)
chante: house or home
chavalo: young kid or boy
chavos: guys
chiva: heroin (*slang*)
cholo: teenage member of a gang in the barrio
chucos: short for *Pachucos*
cocina: kitchen
compas: friends
corridos: a song in Spanish that tells a story
cuates: buddy or buddies
cuidao: be careful, watch out
curandera: folk healer

embrujo: bewitched

gabachos: gringos or Anglos

huesos: bones

jefa: mother
jefito: father
la jura: the cop
jaina: girlfriend

llano: prairie or plains
La Llorona: the weeper that roams ditches
locotes: crazy dudes
locos: crazy dudes

manta: blanket or shawl
Mejicles: Mexico (*slang*)
mestizo: person of Mexican/Indian blood descent

niño: child

pelo rojo: marijuana
perros: dogs
pozole: native hominy

Quarai: ancient mission ruins in Punta de Agua, a small pueblo in the Manzano Mountains.

ranflas: nice car

Sanjo: name of a barrio in Albuquerque
santito: little saint

tápalo: woman's head veil
tecatos: heroin addicts
tiendita: little store
Tijerina's courthouse raid: on June 5, 1967, a group of armed men took over the courthouse in the mountain village of Tierra Amarilla, New Mexico, as a protest against violations of their civil rights. They were men of the Alianza, headed by Reies López Tijerina.
Torreón: pueblo in Manzano Mountains

vatos: guys
viejos: old people
viga: beam or joist

New Directions Paperbooks—A Partial Listing

Walter Abish, *How German Is It.* NDP508.
John Allman, *Scenarios for a Mixed Landscape.* NDP619.
Sherwood Anderson, *Poor White.* NDP763.
Wayne Andrews, *The Surrealist Parade.* NDP689.
David Antin, *Tuning.* NDP570.
G. Apollinaire, *Selected Writings.†* NDP310.
Jimmy S. Baca, *Martín & Meditations.* NDP648.
  Black Mesa Poems. NDP676.
Djuna Barnes, *Nightwood.* NDP98.
J. Barzun, *An Essay on French Verse.* NDP708.
H.E. Bates, *Elephant's Nest in a Rhubarb Tree.* NDP669.
  A Party for the Girls, NDP653.
Charles Baudelaire, *Flowers of Evil.†* NDP684.
  Paris Spleen. NDP294.
Bei Dao, *Old Snow.* NDP727.
  Waves. NDP693.
Gottfried Benn, *Primal Vision.* NDP322.
Adolfo Bioy Casares, *A Russian Doll.* NDP745.
Carmel Bird, *The Bluebird Café.* NDP707.
R. P. Blackmur, *Studies in Henry James,* NDP552.
Wolfgang Borchert, *The Man Outside.* NDP319.
Jorge Luis Borges, *Labyrinths.* NDP186.
  Seven Nights. NDP576.
Kay Boyle, *Life Being the Best.* NDP654.
  Fifty Stories. NDP741.
M. Bulgakov, *Flight & Bliss.* NDP593.
  The Life of M. de Moliere. NDP601.
Frederick Busch, *Absent Friends.* NDP721.
Veza Canetti, *Yellow Street.* NDP709.
Ernesto Cardenal, *Zero Hour.* NDP502.
Joyce Cary, *A House of Children.* NDP631.
  Mister Johnson. NDP631.
Hayden Carruth, *Tell Me Again. . . .* NDP677.
Louis-Ferdinand Céline,
  Death on the Installment Plan. NDP330.
  Journey to the End of the Night. NDP542.
René Char. *Selected Poems.†* NDP734.
Jean Cocteau, *The Holy Terrors.* NDP212.
M. Collis, *She Was a Queen.* NDP716.
Cid Corman, *Sun Rock Man.* NDP318.
Gregory Corso, *Long Live Man.* NDP127.
  Herald of the Autochthonic Spirit. NDP522.
Robert Creeley, *Memory Gardens.* NDP613.
  Windows. NDP687.
Edward Dahlberg, *Because I Was Flesh.* NDP227.
Alain Daniélou, *The Way to the Labyrinth.* NDP634.
Osamu Dazai, *The Setting Sun.* NDP258.
  No Longer Human. NDP357.
Mme. de Lafayette, *The Princess of Cleves.* NDP660.
E. Dujardin, *We'll to the Woods No More.* NDP682.
Robert Duncan, *Selected Poems.* NDP754.
Richard Eberhart, *The Long Reach.* NDP565.
Wm. Empson, *7 Types of Ambiguity.* NDP204.
  Some Versions of Pastoral. NDP92.
S. Endo, *The Sea and the Poison.* NDP737.
Wm. Everson, *The Residual Years.* NDP263.
Gavin Ewart, *Selected Poems.* NDP655.
Lawrence Ferlinghetti, *A Coney Island of
  the Mind.* NDP74.
  Starting from San Francisco. NDP220.
  Wild Dreams of a New Beginning. NDP663.
Ronald Firbank, *Five Novels.* NDP581.
  Three More Novels. NDP614.
F. Scott Fitzgerald, *The Crack-up.* NDP54.
Gustave Flaubert, *Dictionary.* NDP230.
J. Gahagan, *Did Gustav Mahler Ski?* NDP711.
Gandhi, *Gandhi on Non-Violence.* NDP197.
Gary, Romain, *Promise at Dawn.* NDP635.
  The Life Before Us ("Madame Rosa"). NDP604.
W. Gerhardie, *Futility.* NDP722.
Goethe, *Faust,* Part I. NDP70.
Allen Grossman, *The Ether Dome.* NDP723.
Martin Grzimek, *Shadowlife.* NDP705.
Guignonat, Henri, *Daemon in Lithuania.* NDP592.
Lars Gustafsson, *The Death of a Beekeeper.* NDP523.
  A Tiler's Afternoon. NDP761.

John Hawkes, *The Beetle Leg.* NDP239.
  Humors of Blood & Skin. NDP577.
  Second Skin. NDP146.
Samuel Hazo, *To Paris.* NDP512.
H. D. *Collected Poems.* NDP611.
  Helen in Egypt. NDP380.
  HERmione. NDP526.
  Selected Poems. NDP658.
  Tribute to Freud. NDP572.
Robert E. Helbling, *Heinrich von Kleist.* NDP390.
William Herrick, *Bradovich.* NDP762.
Herman Hesse, *Siddhartha.* NDP65.
Paul Hoover, *The Novel.* NDP706.
Susan Howe, *The Nonconformist's Memorial.* NDP755.
Vicente Huidobro, *Selected Poetry.* NDP520.
C. Isherwood, *All the Conspirators.* NDP480.
  The Berlin Stories. NDP134.
Ledo Ivo, *Snake's Nest.* NDP521.
Fleur Jaeggy, *Sweet Days of Discipline.* NDP758.
Gustav Janouch, *Conversations with Kafka.* NDP313.
Alfred Jarry, *Ubu Roi.* NDP105.
Robinson Jeffers, *Cawdor and Medea.* NDP293.
B.S. Johnson, *Christie Malry's. . . .* NDP600.
  Albert Angelo. NDP628.
James Joyce, *Stephen Hero.* NDP133.
Franz Kafka, *Amerika.* NDP117.
Mary Karr, *The Devil's Tour.* NDP768.
Bob Kaufman, *The Ancient Rain.* NDP514.
H. von Kleist, *Prince Friedrich.* NDP462.
Rüdiger Kremer, *The Color of Snow.* NDP743.
Jules Laforgue, *Moral Tales.* NDP594.
P. Lal, *Great Sanskrit Plays.* NDP142.
Tommaso Landolfi, *Gogol's Wife.* NDP155.
"Language" Poetries: An Anthology. NDP630.
D. Larsen, *Stitching Porcelain.* NDP710.
James Laughlin, *The Man in the Wall.* NDP759.
Lautréamont, *Maldoror.* NDP207.
H. Leibowitz, *Fabricating Lives.* NDP715.
Siegfried Lenz, *The German Lesson.* NDP618.
Denise Levertov, *Breathing the Water.* NDP640.
  A Door in the Hive. NDP685.
  Evening Train. NDP750.
  New & Selected Essays. NDP749.
  Poems 1960-1967. NDP549.
  Poems 1968-1972. NDP629.
  Oblique Prayers. NDP578.
Harry Levin, *James Joyce.* NDP87.
Li Ch'ing-chao, *Complete Poems.* NDP492.
Enrique Lihn, *The Dark Room.†* NDP542.
C. Lispector, *Soulstorm.* NDP671.
  The Hour of the Star. NDP733.
Garciá Lorca, *Five Plays.* NDP232.
  The Public & Play Without a Title. NDP561.
  Selected Poems.† NDP114.
  Three Tragedies. NDP52.
Francisco G. Lorca, *In The Green Morning.* NDP610.
Michael McClure, *Rebel Lions.* NDP712.
  Selected Poems. NDP599.
Carson McCullers, *The Member of the
  Wedding.* (Playscript) NDP153.
Stéphane Mallarme,† *Selected Poetry and
  Prose.* NDP529.
Bernadette Mayer, *A Bernadette Mayer Reader.* NDP739.
Thomas Merton, *Asian Journal.* NDP394.
  New Seeds of Contemplation. ND337.
  Selected Poems. NDP85.
  Thomas Merton in Alaska. NDP652.
  The Way of Chuang Tzu. NDP276.
  Zen and the Birds of Appetite. NDP261.
Henri Michaux, *A Barbarian in Asia.* NDP622.
  Selected Writings. NDP264.
Henry Miller, *The Air-Conditioned Nightmare.*
  NDP302.
  Aller Retour New York. NDP753.
  Big Sur & The Oranges. NDP161.
  The Colossus of Maroussi. NDP75.
  A Devil in Paradise. NDP765.
  Into the Heart of Life. NDP728.
  The Smile at the Foot of the Ladder. NDP386.

For complete listing request free catalog from
New Directions, 80 Eighth Avenue, New York 10011

†Bilingual

For complete listing request free catalog from
New Directions, 80 Eighth Avenue, New York 10011

†Bilingual

force in my life—create a better world, a better me,
out of love. I became a child of the house,
and it showed me
the freedom of a new beginning.

*   *   *   *